Lincolns at worl

on old picture postcards

Eric Croft

1. Burton-upon-Stather. A blacksmith is shoeing a rather placid-looking shire horse. Photographer was Eric Wood of Burton, but the card is not dated. However, the trade directory for 1912 gives the blacksmith as a Mr. William Wood, who was also clerk to the parish council and a rate collector!

**Printed by
Adlard Print and Typesetting Services,
Ruddington, Notts.**

£3.50

LINCOLNSHIRE AT WORK

Locations featured in the book

2. A scene at **Frodingham,** near Scunthorpe, with a traction engine belonging to Springs of Brigg entering the station yard. Springs manufactured lemon curd so perhaps these men were collecting a load of lemons or sugar. This postcard was posted at Scunthorpe in April 1907. The engine is a Burrell single crank compound.

3. Scunthorpe. Quarrying ironstone with the steelworks in the background. The scene is undated but is probably in the early 1930s. The steam-driven excavator was manufactured by Rustons of Lincoln.

INTRODUCTION

The picture postcards featured in this book provide a selection of illustrations of people at work in Lincolnshire, mostly before 1920. The rural nature of the county is reflected in many of the scenes, though engineering and heavier industries are also represented. The labour-intensive nature of much business is evident in an age when agricultural jobs were steadily diminishing, to be replaced by work in factories, on the railways, or in shipbuilding. Traditional roles for women in domestic service were also becoming less important as they were attracted by higher wages into shops, mills and offices. World War One accelerated this process because of a shortage of male labour, and women increasingly went into nursing, welfare and education, as well as factory and transport work.

In Edwardian times, skilled male workers could expect to earn around thirty shillings a week, which was often supplemented by overtime. Despite pockets of extreme poverty, living standards generally rose in the period as food prices tended to fall.

Picture postcards were first published in Britain in 1894, but it was not until 1902, when the Post Office allowed the message to be written on the back alongside the address, that they became really popular. Both national and local publishers issued views of scenes, events and people that have given us a marvellous legacy of pictures from the Edwardian era. Where known, card publishers have been acknowledged, though many of these featured in this book were published anonymously, probably in small numbers.

Eric Croft
May 1995

**Designed and published by
Reflections of a Bygone Age,
Keyworth, Nottingham 1995**
Reprinted 1997, 2000, 2003

ISBN 0 946245 97 5

If any readers have postcards or photographs, or other information which might be useful for future publications, please contact me at 80 Yarborough Crescent, Lincoln (01522-539955).

Back cover (top): roadworkers at **Swinderby** in a somewhat posed photograph in the 1930s.

(bottom): Swineshead windmill in its hey-day about 1910. The mill ceased production in the 1930s, and after years of standing derelict is now being restored.

4. Grimsby. From the hundreds of views of the fish market here, it seems there must have been as many photographers as fishermen there! Card published about 1910 by Shaw of Grimsby: obviously the large cod got individual treatment with the smaller ones dumped into boxes.

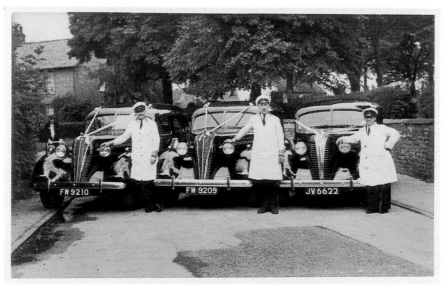

5. Chauffeurs from W.D. Fothergill's garage at **Cleethorpes** dressed in white on wedding days. 1930s view features three cars from the 'Royal Garage' fleet.

S.S. CALEDONIAN, LONDON.

Size—178 × 26·3 × 11·3   Gross Tons—513.

REPAIRED BY CHARLTON & DOUGHTY, LTD.,

On their No. 2 6 Working Days.

6. Grimsby ship repairers Charlton & Doughty were proud of their achievement in refurbishing *SS Caledonian* from London in five working days. Reverse of the card was pre-printed for correspondence; it was published by Lowther Bros. of Grimsby.

7. Workmen felling a tree at **Brigg** long before the chain saw. The card was published by Grayson Clarke of Brigg about 1910.

8. Grasby. Shopkeepers Mr. & Mrs. Ward on the steps of their village store. Apart from being 'grocers, drapers and dealers in tobaccos', other goods in the windows include dolls, toy cars, lamps and clocks. A typical postcard from the Edwardian period.

9. Immingham. Admiralty cable workers binding the loop on cable at the docks in 1920.

10. Teaching science at **Caistor** Grammar School c.1920, a mixed school as was usual in small towns. The school now has grant-maintained status (and hopefully a new laboratory!). Card published by Marshall, Keene & Co. of Hove, who specialised in postcards for schools.

11. Haxey and Owston Ferry Pumping Station construction.

12. Road workers – and the ever-present tar boiler on this job – at **Fulstow** in 1912, with local roadman Sam Bradley in the centre.

13. Osgodby, near Market Rasen. A lovely card of Robinson's engineering shop about 1920. Mr. Robinson was a threshing machine owner, so presumably the Marshall of Gainsborough machine on the left was his own. The engine in the foreground is an Aveling Porter.

S 4950   MARSHALLS WORKS. GAINSBOROUGH.

14. Gainsborough, and a view of Marshall's engineering works. This card was published by W.H. Smith and posted at Retford in September 1915. Alas, like so many other Lincolnshire engineering companies, Marshall's are no longer in business.

15. More road works, this time near **Gainsborough,** with the workmen on lunch break. Anonymously-published card from the 1930s.

16. Willingham-by-Stow. A postcard showing local butcher Mr. Foottit on his round in 1906. 5^1/$_2$ miles south-east of Gainsborough, the village had a population of about 400 at this time.

17. Owmby-by-Spital. Another group of council roadmen with their horse-drawn tar boiler. The signpost indicates that the photograph, of c.1912 vintage, was taken at the road junction between Normanby and Owmby.

18. Louth. Council workmen in what appears to be their local depot: the cart is clearly marked 'Louth Corporation'. Postcard published by E.F. Blaze of Louth, and posted to Grimsby in June 1911. The message doesn't mention the view – hardly a best-seller!

19. The blacksmith's shop at **Lissington.** The card was sent to Sleaford in September 1907 with the quaint message *"I am sending you a view and its puzzle – find the dear old blacksmith."* Alfred Cundill was the gentleman in question.

20. Welton. This card, posted from the village in July 1905, shows Mr. Gilbert outside his premises. He'd sent this postcard to a gentleman in Market Rasen: *"I have several cart collars lined by other saddlers coming to the establishment for alterations. If you require anything done you will receive my best attention."*

21. Most villages had their own blacksmith's shop but **Nettleham** was obviously busier than most, with five men employed in the 1920s.

22. Signalman Walter Prescott on the steps of **East Barkwith** signal box. He was so proud of his box he paid for the photograph to be taken by Lincoln photographer R. Horner. This card was posted in September 1915.

23. East Barkwith. Four painters posing for the photographer at the level crossing in the 1930s. The village, 3½ miles north-east of Wragby, had a turn-of-the-century population of 307, and contained nursery grounds and manure works.

24. Saxilby. This farm cart needed all three horses as it appears to be loaded with roof tiles! The card was owned by Charles Paddison of Ingleby, and the man on the right is his foreman Jack Marrison. The photo is of c.1912 vintage.

25. Saxilby. Barges were a common sight on the Fosse Dyke canal until fairly recent times. This 1920s view features the "Belle of the Trent" with bargee George Marrison.

26. Lincoln. A photo of Lincoln Corporation dustmen in the St. Giles area of the city about 1920, with a Lincoln-made electric wagon from Clayton and Shuttleworth.

27. Smalley & Son's shop and delivery cart at 373 High rounding district. Note the prominent sign for 'oysters' an a young lad. This fine card probably dates from c.1915.

SMALLEY & SON,
FRUITERER
FISH, GAME AND POULTRY
— DEALER —

Telephone № 35.

incoln. The firm had several shops in the city and sur-
phone number on the cart (35!), which is being driven by

28. A tram conductor at **Lincoln** in the early 1930s.

29. Lincoln. Another couple of dustmen in the Burton Road area, but this time with a one-horse-power cart, about 1912.

30. Lincoln. A trailer-load of tarpaulins leaving Singleton and Flint's works in 1916. The company is still making waterproof covers in the city.

THE DESTRUCTION OF THE OLD CHIMNEY
AT DAWBER'S BREWERY, LINCOLN.
P. JONES. LINCOLN. 20/2/07.

31. Carholme Road, **Lincoln,** in 1907. The caption provides all the details of the event. A similar card informs us that the demolition was carried out by Otters, a local firm which is no longer in business. Neither is the brewery! The postcard was published by P. Jones.

32. Lincoln. Policemen on parade in the grounds of the old Sessions House/police station on Monks Road, probably in the 1920s. Card publisher was Frisby of Lincoln.

33. This is one of several cards published by Lincoln photographer Harrison during the First World War of ward scenes at **Lincoln** Northern Military Hospital, based at Lincoln Christ's Hospital School on Wragby Road.

34. Bracebridge Heath, and builders renovating a local pub. Instead of the building firm's advertising board, the most prominent sign is for *'Mowbray & Co., noted Grantham Ales'.* The card was sent to Minnie Walker at Mablethorpe by Alf, who wondered *"if you know anyone on it."* It was posted in September 1909.

35. North Hykeham. Workers at Harrison's iron factory with a display of the company's products. The foundry has had many names over the years but was known by many people as "The Malleable". The works are still producing castings under the name of George Fischer (Lincoln) Ltd. Card published by W.R. Moore of Sheffield about 1910.

36. Aby, three miles north-west of Alford. The blacksmith's shop on a card posted in 1912. The machinery on view includes a hay rake, reaper, and sets of harrows. Mr. Marfleet was blacksmith at the time.

37. Hagworthingham, and a card showing thatch being stripped from a derelict cottage. Mr. Dracass, who published this card, was listed as grocer and postmaster in 1912. He produced several postcards around this time, mostly well-animated but all very dull in appearance.

38. Pumping out water from the "Punch House" at **Horncastle,** with the urban district council's hand-operated fire engine. The flood was the result of a severe cloudburst on May 30th 1920. The same storm was dramatically more severe at Louth, where the town was engulfed, killing 24 people and making over a thousand homeless.

MAREHAM ON THE HILL DAIRY FARM. L. WINGATE - PROPRIETOR.
ORDERS LEFT AT 31 EAST STREET, HORNCASTLE, WILL BE PROMPTLY DELIVERED.

39. Mareham on the Hill. This postcard, sent to a village near Boston in November 1910, shows a proud Mr. Wingate in a very contrived advertising photograph complete with dairy boy and milkmaid. Presumably he owned more than the one cow!

40. Woodhall Spa. Nurses at the Petwood Hotel, which was used as a military hospital during the First World War. The card was published by A. Blades of Horncastle, who produced many fine photographic postcards of the area.

41. Eagle. Forestry workers – including a number of women – in the 1914-18 period on a card published by Thomas Hoe of Collingham.

42. Carlton-le-Moorland, with a typical. carrier's cart. This one belonged to A. Harwood, who advertised himself as a 'Newark and Lincoln carrier'. The postcard was published by Hunt & Co. of Newark about 1920, but despite the early date the cart features exterior advertising (for Hudson's soap and Wyles Bros.' boots).

43. Bardney Abbey is recorded as having been destroyed by the Danes in 870 and rebuilt by William the Conqueror. Excavations were carried out in 1912, but it was obviously local and fairly amateurish. The Rev. Laing was the local vicar, Mr. Crowder a corn dealer, and Mr. Clipsham the village plumber! This card was one of a long series published by Ruddocks of Lincoln.

44. Bardney Windmill on a postcard sent to Market Rasen in October 1912. The owners at this time were Varlow and Blanshard, who were not only millers and dealers in agricultural products but owned four farms in the area. Like most of the Lincolnshire windmills, only the brick tower remains today.

45. Skegness. W. Brown's grocer van from Wainfleet Road grocery stores. The advert on the side of the van also mentions that the shop was an agent for Whitbread Ales and Stouts. In 1912, Mr. Brown owned two shops in the town – the other on Lumley Road.

46. The Samuel Lewis Lifeboat and crew at **Skegness** on a card posted to Caistor in November 1917. The message from a lady in Spilsby barely mentions the lifeboat, but she is complaining that *"we can't get a currant in Spilsby"* – presumably because of the war.

47. Coningsby. A bread delivery cart in the late 1940s, on a card published by E.R. Dixon of Lincoln. Rowell's business had been established in the village for at least half a century.

48. Billinghay. The village fire brigade at practice in 1919 on a postcard by Upton of Sleaford. Perhaps – judging by the large number of onlookers – they didn't practise very often!

49. Sleaford. Workers queueing up on payday at malsters Bass, Ratcliffe and Gretton Ltd. about 1912. The site now houses some industrial units, but some of the Victorian buildings were severely damaged in a fire a few years ago; so far they have not been demolished. Hopefully, they will be restored and put to a practical use.

50. Belton, near Grantham. A group of joiners pose for their photograph while building the army camp in Belton Park in 1914. Nearly all have collars and ties, and many have flat caps – except for the foreman in his bowler. Postcard published by T. Burnett of Middlesbrough.

51. Oasby. A lovely farmyard scene; but Mr. Fisher Wakefield, whose name is on the wagon, is not listed in any trade directory as a farmer, but as the landlord of the "Houblon Arms."

52. Grantham. The town's fire brigade pictured on a postcard by Simpson & Son of that town. Several of the firemen are wearing medals, so perhaps this was part of a parade in the 1930s.

53. The delivery cart of **Grantham** brewers Mowbray in St. Catherine's Road, seen on a card published by Walter Lee of London Road, Grantham. One of the draymen was a Mr. Clayton.

54. Boston. A superb postcard of Simpson & Son's Aveling steam wagon with trailers outside their premises at 22 Market Place. The steam wagon had originally been owned by G.H. Kent of Maud Street saw mill, but their name has been crudely painted out.

55. Portrait of a postman at **Stamford** c.1915. The helmet-style cap and brass-buttoned waistcoat and jacket give him an almost military look.

56. Grantham. W.C. Warrener's coal delivery service in the pre-1914 era.

57. Surfleet. The blacksmith's shop on Station Road c.1910. An added piece of Lincolnshire history is one of the ploughs, made by Barlow's of Kirkby Lathorpe.